Developing
Professional Skills:
BUSINESS
ASSOCIATIONS

Michelle M. Harner

Professor of Law, Co-Director Business Law Professor
University of Maryland Francis King Carey School of Law

Series Editor
Colleen Medill

MAT # 41232780

© 2012 Thomson Reuters
        610 Opperman Drive
        St. Paul, MN 55123
        1-800-313-9378

Printed in the United States of America

ISBN: 9-780-314-27960-6

This book is dedicated to
Paul, Nate, Zach, Alex and Maria

Preface

LAW SCHOOLS TODAY aspire to teach professional legal skills. The current emphasis on skills training is in response to the criticism that the traditional law school curriculum does not adequately train students to practice law. The high cost of law school tuition, coupled with the tight job market for law school graduates in recent years, has intensified the demand for more skills training in law schools.

Incorporating skills training into doctrinal law courses is challenging. Elaborate simulations can crowd out the coverage of fundamental legal concepts and doctrines, leaving both the professor and the students frustrated. The professor feels that there is never enough time to cover the subject matter adequately. The students feel that there is never enough time, period.

Developing Professional Skills: Business Associations is designed to provide skills training to law students in a time-efficient manner. Each chapter in this book focuses on one of the following four core legal skills:

- ▶ Client Counseling (including engagement of a new client, interviewing and fact gathering);

- ▶ Legal Drafting (including client correspondence via letters and e-mails as well as traditional legal document drafting);

- ▶ Negotiation; and

- ▶ Advocacy.

Students are expected to spend about one to two hours outside of the classroom preparing the skills assignment for each chapter.
A comprehensive Teacher's Manual gives the professor both guidance and discretion in determining how much classroom discussion time to devote to the material in each chapter. The professor may spend a brief amount of time reviewing the "answer" to the problem presented in the chapter. Or, the professor may expand the discussion to include concepts of professional responsibility and the norms of modern legal practice. Suggestions for incorporating professional responsibility concepts and the norms of legal practice into the classroom discussion are contained in the Teacher's Manual. For professors who desire to expand the scope of a skills exercise, selected provisions of the *Model Rules of Professional Conduct* and client time sheets are reproduced as Appendix material at the end of the book.

Developing Professional Skills: Business Associations is intended to bring to life the materials taught in the basic Business Associations course. The standard classroom routine of reading cases and answering questions generally is not what students envision when they enter law school. As lawyers, students will encounter idiosyncratic, demanding, and occasionally unreasonable clients, constantly evolving new technology, old-fashioned financial and time management constraints, and most of all, interesting problems to solve. Importantly, they will then be asked to implement their solutions to those problems. Although no book can truly simulate the nuanced tapestry that is modern legal practice, the skills exercises in this book can be used to enhance and enrich the students' educational experience and lead them a significant step closer to being practicing lawyers and legal counselors.

Several generous friends provided support and willingly shared their expertise to assist me in the writing of this book. First and foremost, I thank Colleen Medill, Warren R. Wise Professor of Law at the University of Nebraska and the creator and primary force behind the *Developing Professional Skills* series, for her support, encouragement and invitation to participate in this important project. I also thank Louis Higgins, Editor in Chief at West Academic Publishing, for giving me the opportunity to contribute to the series. Dean Phoebe Haddon and the University of Maryland Francis King Carey School of Law provided both expertise and financial support for this project. Several of my colleagues at the University of Maryland and other academic institutions graciously shared their knowledge and experiences with me for purposes of this book, including Robert Condlin, Jessica Erickson, Daniel Goldberg, Jason Hawkins, Jennifer Ivey-Crickenberger, Alice Johnson, Wulf Kaal, Sheldon Krantz, Robert Rhee and Brian Sawers. In addition, a number of practitioners offered insights and experiences that proved invaluable as I wrote this book; they are too many to name here, but I certainly am grateful to them all.

Michelle M. Harner
August, 2012

Introduction

Developing Professional Skills: Business Associations introduces you to the variety of skills that differentiate the law student from the experienced legal practitioner. Like any type of skill, acquiring professional legal skills takes time and patience, but most of all, it takes practice. Each chapter in this book provides you with the opportunity to practice a legal skill that you are likely to use again and again after you graduate from law school.

The chapters of this book are organized according to topics that usually are covered in the basic Business Associations course. In Chapter One, you encounter a prospective client who wants to part ways with his business partner and needs your counseling. In Chapter Two, you must draft an advisory letter to two clients concerning the potential entity choices for forming their new business venture. In Chapter Three, you meet up with a childhood friend who needs your help in evaluating and negotiating a buy-sell agreement. Chapter Four requires you to draft a certificate of incorporation for a start-up entity. In Chapter Five, you will prepare a motion to dismiss a complaint in the context of a breach of fiduciary duty lawsuit against the directors of your corporate client. Chapter Six asks you to respond to a sensitive e-mail from a director of your corporate client proposing an interested director transaction. In Chapter Seven, you represent disgruntled shareholders and must prepare a demand letter to the corporation's board of directors. Chapter Eight involves the negotiation of an indemnification agreement for a corporate officer. In Chapter Nine, you are hired as counsel to the board of directors in connection with the company's proposed sale of substantially all of its assets. Finally, in Chapter Ten, you are asked to draft a voting agreement for three minority shareholders. Client counseling, legal drafting, negotiation and advocacy are the core skills of the legal profession. *Developing Professional Skills: Business Associations* provides you with the opportunity to begin to acquire these skills.

Table of Contents

Developing Professional Skills:
BUSINESS ASSOCIATIONS

CHAPTER ONE

Partnership Formation and Dissolution
Breaking Up Is Hard to Do

AS YOU SIT IN YOUR OFFICE reading *The Wall Street Journal,* your assistant asks if you have time to talk to a prospective client. Although people do not typically show up at your door without at least calling first to make an appointment, your calendar is light this particular morning and you are always open to discussing new business. You ask your assistant to bring the prospective client up to your office.

A young man (looks to be in his twenties) in jeans and a blazer with disheveled hair walks in and takes a seat. He looks anxious and concerned—almost too distracted to speak. You initiate the conversation with some small talk:

> *You:* Good morning. It's a beautiful day out there, don't you think?
>
> *Young Man:* I didn't notice. (Dead silence.)
>
> *You:* I apologize but I didn't quite catch your name or what brings you into my office today.
>
> *Young Man:* My name is Michael Quinn, and I am having some trouble with my business partner. My aunt said you could help me.
>
> *You:* Your aunt—who is that?
>
> *Young Man:* Sheila Quinn. She said that you were the best business lawyer in town and could get me out of my current situation. And she said not to worry about your fees and expenses; she will take care of them.

You know Sheila Quinn. She owns Quinn Consultants, a financial advisory firm, and she is one of your best and favorite clients. You make a quick note to thank Sheila for the referral and vote of confidence. You then get down to business.

Michael has been trying to start a business with his college roommate, Ben Street. You are having a hard time getting your head around their business concept, and it appears that you are not alone. Michael and Ben have failed to attract any investors. Michael explains that lack of adequate funding and disagreements between him and Ben over product design have stalled product development and marketing.

You are intrigued by this representation and would like to do it, in part to please Sheila. You must tread carefully in this initial conversation, however, until you ascertain whether the representation of this new client would present a conflict with your representation of existing clients. You ask Michael about other parties involved with the business, including any suppliers, vendors or other people they may owe money. Michael indicates that it is just him and Ben, but that he personally has invested and lost a lot of money, which is why his aunt is helping him get back on his feet. You take Michael to get a cup of coffee in the office kitchen while your assistant does a preliminary conflicts check on the only other known party in the matter, Ben Street. This preliminary conflicts check indicates that you may represent Michael. Although you still need to hammer out the terms of the engagement letter with Michael, you feel more comfortable proceeding with the discussion.

Michael explains that he and Ben came up with this "crazy" idea to create a voice recognition program that would translate your daily life into a written memoir. The concept, as you understand it, involves a small ear piece that acts as an electronic dictation device so that it records and translates to a digital file everything you and those around you say during the course of a day. The duo apparently came up with the idea late one night when they were bemoaning the ambiguity of their class notes and the term paper they had to write. They had the solution—this small device would do the work for them.

Unfortunately, Michael invested most of his savings in the business, and the concept has yet to materialize or generate the investor and market excitement they had anticipated. Investors apparently keep raising "nonsensical" (Michael's word, not yours) concerns about privacy and related litigation and liability. You ask Michael about the terms of the business relationship between him and Ben. He responds that they are partners and had been working together really well until Michael ran out of money and asked Ben to make an investment. They have barely spoken since that communication. Michael wants his money back. He also wants to find a new business partner who can develop the concept into a commercial success.

Your assistant interrupts your conversation with Michael to remind you of a lunch meeting in the main conference room. You apologize to Michael and explain that you need to attend a previously scheduled meeting. You suggest that Michael schedule another appointment with your assistant for the end of the week, at which time you hope to have formal conflicts clearance and an engagement letter for Michael to review and sign. You also ask Michael to send you any correspondence or materials relating to the business. Michael says that he only kept a few e-mails and promises to forward the e-mails before the next meeting. He asks if you will be able to give him some guidance on how to proceed at that meeting. You respond that you will do your best.

When you arrive at your office the next morning, you find a flurry of e-mails from Michael. The following e-mail catches your eye:

To: Michael Quinn
From: Ben Street <bstreet@isp.com>
Subject: Lame, Really LAME!

Mike:

I can't believe you're bailing on me. You promised to provide the cash, and I was going to provide the talent. We were going to make millions together and split everything right down the middle. Well, I don't need your money. I will just take my idea and find a new partner—someone who understands the value of my concept and shares my vision.

— Ben

You then check your voice mails; one is from Michael. He says that he will see you in two days and that his Aunt Sheila is coming to the meeting.

Luckily, your morning conference call has been cancelled, so you begin preparing for the meeting. You quickly realize that you have several significant issues to discuss with Michael and perhaps Sheila. You take a deep breath and then begin methodically to prepare a talking points outline, which is helpful for important meetings and negotiations. This method has never failed you before, and you certainly need it now.

Prepare for your next meeting with Michael and Sheila by using the "Who-What-Why-How" approach to problem solving. Use the *Client Counseling Outline* reproduced at the end of Chapter One to practice this client counseling technique.

Points to Consider:

1. Are Michael and Ben partners? Does Michael want to characterize his business relationship with Ben as a partnership? If their business relationship is not a partnership, what is it?

2. Do we need to consider how Michael's accountant has been reporting these expenditures on Michael's tax returns? Who owns the concept? Does Michael have any rights to the concept? Does Michael have any liability here?

3. Can you discuss all of these issues with Michael while his Aunt Sheila is in the room? Does it matter that she is paying your legal fees and expenses?

Client Counseling Outline

Attorney Name:

Client:

Date:

WHO is involved in the new matter?

WHAT facts present potential problem(s) in the matter?

As described by client:

As perceived by you:

Client Counseling Outline, continued

WHY do these facts present potential problems?

HOW should you address the potential problems?

CHAPTER TWO

Entity Choice
A Tasty Investment Opportunity

BETH RUNS A SMALL catering business in town, and she frequently caters events at your law firm. Her food is exquisite, reasonably priced and always comes with terrific customer service. She is well-known throughout the legal and business communities, and she has become the go-to caterer for corporate luncheons and law firm receptions. She earned further fame by winning a cooking competition on a national television program.

Beth is at a critical point in her business operations. She is underfunded and understaffed. As a result, she is turning away business. She cringes at the thought of all the money she is losing because of these missed opportunities.

Fortunately for Beth, her television appearance and her use of social media have spread her fame far and wide. Nonetheless, she is surprised when she receives a call from a well-known financial investor, Andrew Fund, to cater a dinner for his family, friends and loyal clients. Beth explains to Andrew that she would love to accept the engagement, but she simply does not have the capacity to do it. Andrew is surprised to hear that, despite Beth's success, she is so cash-strapped and thinly staffed. Beth explains that she and her best friend from college, Cheryl, started the business together on dreams and a shoestring, with Beth doing all of the cooking and Cheryl handling the marketing and scheduling aspects of the business. The business took off more quickly than either of them had expected, and they never stopped to consider how best to fund the business or move it forward.

During their conversation, Andrew asked Beth if she would consider sharing her business plan with him. Beth said that she would be happy to do so, if she only knew what a business plan was. Andrew explained that a business plan helps business owners evaluate their operational and funding needs in light of things like operating costs, anticipated growth and projected revenues. Beth explained that she and Cheryl track income and expenses and that she includes these items in her personal income tax returns. When Andrew expressed some surprise that Beth and Cheryl were not partners or otherwise operating the business as a corporation, Beth responded that Cheryl had just been helping her out with her cooking hobby. Neither one of them expected to be running a business.

Sensing opportunity, Andrew suggested that Beth stop by his office for a meeting later that week. Beth assumed that he wanted to sample some of her catering menu, so she reminded him that she would not be able to cater his event. Andrew said that he actually had a business proposition for her to help fund and grow her catering business. Beth was intrigued and agreed to the meeting.

At the meeting, Andrew presented Beth with a letter in which he proposed to make an initial investment of $250,000 in Beth's catering business in exchange for a fifty-percent ownership interest. The letter explained that Andrew and Beth would work together to expand the business by, among other things, leasing space in a commercial kitchen, employing additional staff to help with food preparation and delivery and buying customized delivery trucks. The letter indicated that Andrew, through one or more of his business associates, would manage the business side of things, leaving Beth to manage the food selection, preparation and presentation aspects. Andrew commented that this type of arrangement would allow each to utilize her or his unique skills sets to enhance the overall business.

Beth was not quite sure how to respond to Andrew's proposal. She had never contemplated a business partner. She also was concerned about how Cheryl, who had been so loyal to Beth throughout the years, would perceive the proposed arrangement. Beth expressed her concerns about Cheryl, as well as her hesitation to turn her hobby and passion into a full-time job with a complete stranger as a partner. Andrew assured her that they could make this work and suggested that they develop a list of objectives together to guide their business endeavor. They produced the following list:

Beth's Objectives:
- Maintain focus on quality products and service
- Retain some control of business and operations
- Recognize and reward Cheryl's loyalty
- Invest/risk only a small amount of capital (to protect what little savings she has)
- Receive enough income to allow her to make the business more than a hobby

Andrew's Objectives:
- Obtain some control of business and operations
- Pursue a growth strategy for business
- Achieve above-market returns on investment
- Maximize upside potential and minimize downside risk
- Retain ability to use losses incurred by new venture for tax purposes
- Receive flexibility on duration of investment and available exit strategies

Your law firm has represented Andrew in a number of matters. The partner at your firm who oversees and bills all legal work done for Andrew stops by your office and hands you Andrew's and Beth's list of objectives. He gives you some additional background on the proposed business venture, and asks you to draft an advisory letter explaining the business entity alternatives for forming this company. Your letter must be completed by Monday. The billing partner for Andrew gives you one final instruction as he leaves your office: "Make sure you protect Andrew's interests because he is one of the firm's biggest clients."

So much for your Friday night plans. You order in some dinner and get to work.

Prepare the correspondence to Beth and Andrew using the Advisory letter reproduced at the end of Chapter Two.

 Points to Consider:

1. What is the range of primary entity form options for Beth and Andrew given their desire for limited liability? What key attributes for each type of form best suit their objectives?

2. What recommendation for a primary entity form will you make to Beth and Andrew? Does the partner's directive to give particular attention to protecting Andrew's interests change your analysis? Should it?

3. Can you be the lawyer for Beth, Andrew and the yet-to-be-formed entity?

Advisory Letter

Formation Law Firm, LLP
Creative Lawyers for Business Innovation
1000 Alternatives Lane,
City, State 00000

_____, 20_____

Confidential Attorney-Client Communication

Via Electronic Mail

Beth Cook
3 Venture Circle
City, State 00000
bcook@email.com

Andrew Fund
10 Investment Lane
City, State 00000
afund@email.com

Re: Entity Alternatives for Proposed Business Venture

Dear Ms. Cook and Mr. Fund:

You have asked our firm to evaluate your options for organizing your
new business venture and to represent each of you in the business
formation process. You have provided us with basic information
concerning the proposed business and your primary objectives in this

Advisory Letter, continued

Ms. Beth Cook & Mr. Andrew Fund
Confidential Attorney-Client Communication
[Date]
Page 2 of 2

endeavor, as reflected in our preliminary analysis below.
Accordingly, this letter summarizes: (i) the legal entity forms in
which you could operate your contemplated business venture; (ii) the
key attributes of each form relevant to your business objectives; and
(iii) our preliminary recommendation based on the facts you have
provided to date.

1. Potential Entity Forms

2. Key Attributes of Each Entity Form

3. <u>Preliminary Recommendation</u>

I look forward to discussing these alternatives with you. Please do not hesitate to call me with any questions or comments.

Sincerely,

CHAPTER THREE

Buy-Sell Agreements
Hoping for the Best, Planning for the Worst

FRANK, JIM AND SUSAN BOLT inherited a fifty-percent ownership interest in their father's hardware business two years ago. The business, Bolt Hardware, LLC ("Bolt"), started out as a small neighborhood handyman store and is now a local powerhouse in the industry. Bolt operates fifteen retail stores in three states. The company owns the land and the buildings for each of its fifteen stores. It finances the majority of its inventory, but has managed to limit its long-term debt obligations. The trio's father ran the company with an iron fist and was masterful at controlling costs. The company also has a vibrant and growing online business.

The company is operated as a manager-managed limited liability company. Jim and Susan have worked for the company for several years and are part of the management committee. The management committee essentially runs the business. Jim functions as the company's president and Susan serves as its treasurer. The other three managers are family friends, but are qualified for their respective positions and have served the company well for many years. Nevertheless, these three managers collectively hold only one-third of the management committee voting power, with Jim and Susan each holding one-third of that vote. The outside managers also have no ownership interests in the company.

Frank never actively participated in the family business. He went to medical school and is an orthopedic surgeon at an area hospital. The only other family member involved in the business is the trio's mother, Anna, who remains a co-owner of the company. Anna owns the other fifty percent of the company's outstanding units, which will pass to Frank, Jim and Susan upon her death.

Frank is comfortable with the current ownership and management structure of the company. He has a great relationship with both Jim and Susan, and he has tremendous confidence in their management skills and judgment (about most things). He has significant doubts, however, about Jim's only son, Joey, who, according to Frank, |is a deadbeat twenty-something living in Jim's basement and spending Jim's money. Although Frank is not certain, he believes that Jim plans to bring Joey on board at the company to groom him to take over Jim's management position and owner-ship interests at some point in the future. Jim apparently has a real soft spot for Joey and fails to see his shortcomings.

You have known Frank, Jim and Susan since childhood, having gone to elementary school together and having spent much of your youth playing in their backyard. You have remained close friends with Frank, who was your college roommate. When Frank went to medical school, you, unable to stomach your undergraduate biology class, opted for law school. During a social lunch, Frank raises his concerns regarding Jim's succession plan for Bolt with you.

Frank provides you with additional information and color on the situation at Bolt. You quickly realize that his concerns may have some validity, and you agree to review the document Frank signed at the time he inherited his ownership interest in the company. Frank is incredibly grateful, and he promises to scan and e-mail you a copy of Bolt's Operating Agreement. You assure Frank that you will review the agreement as soon as possible and consider his alternatives.

When you receive the Operating Agreement, you take some time to review the agreement in its entirety. It is a fairly standard form Operating Agreement under the laws of your jurisdiction, but you do notice a few interesting provisions relating to the election of managers, the transfer of ownership interests and the members' buy-sell rights. You determine that Frank needs to request amendment of these provisions to fully protect his ownership interest in the business.

Using the three relevant sections of the Operating Agreement Provisions reproduced at the end of Chapter Three, "mark up" these sections (i.e., delete or add language) in order to strengthen Frank's position as a nonmanagerial owner of the business, and identify your justifications for the proposed changes. You know that Jim and Susan will not simply take your word for it—particularly if they involve the company's lawyer—so you need to be prepared for that negotiation. You also know that Frank wants to resolve this matter as quickly as possible to preserve family harmony, so you need to consider the reasonableness of your proposed changes, as well as what you absolutely must get to protect Frank and what you can give up to facilitate a deal. Write a brief explanation for each of your proposed amendments using the Proposed Revisions to Operating Agreement form that follows the Operating Agreement Provisions.

Points to Consider:

1. What triggering mechanisms in the buy-sell provision best protect Frank's interests? Does a different or broader right of first refusal help Frank? How might Jim, Susan and Anna object to a proposed amendment of those provisions?

2. Does the allocation of ownership interests upon Anna's death impact Frank's concerns? If so, how might that issue be addressed in the Operating Agreement? Or, should this issue be addressed in a separate agreement?

3. Does your friendship with Jim and Susan impact your representation of Frank in this matter? Have you agreed to represent Frank as a client?

Name:

Operating Agreement Provisions

ARTICLE II - MANAGEMENT

2.1 Managers. The Company will be managed by one or more managers appointed by the members. Any member holding fifty percent or more of the membership interests will appoint a majority of the managers. The remaining managers will be appointed collectively by any members holding less than fifty percent of the membership interests, with each such member voting in accordance with its percentage of the membership interests. The initial management committee will consist of five managers. Each manager will serve until its removal by a vote of members holding at least seventy-five percent of the membership interests or its resignation. Any vacancy on the management committee will be filled by a vote of the members in accordance with this Section 2.1.

ARTICLE VI - TRANSFER OF MEMBERSHIP INTERESTS

6.1 Restrictions on Transfer. No member may transfer, pledge, assign or encumber the member's membership interest without the prior written consent of disinterested members holding fifty percent or more of the disinterested membership interests.

6.2 Conditions Precedent to Transfer. Any purported transfer, pledge, assignment or encumbrance otherwise complying with Section 6.1 will be ineffective unless and until: (a) the transferor provides the Company with notice of the proposed transfer and an opportunity to purchase the member's membership interests on the same terms offered by the proposed transferee, and the Company fails to purchase the membership interests within thirty days of the Company's receipt of such notice; and (b) the transferor and the proposed transferee furnish to the Company the instruments and assurances the managers may request to confirm the proposed transferee's ability to perform all obligations of members under this Agreement.

ARTICLE VII - BUY-SELL

8.1 Buy-Sell Event. Each of the following events shall constitute a "Buy-Sell Event" for purposes of this Agreement: (a) the death or declaration of legal incompetence of a member; (b) the bankruptcy or a judicial determination of the insolvency of a member; and (c) any withdrawal by a member from the Company or transfer of a membership interest by a member other than as may be expressly permitted by this Agreement.

8.2 Rights Upon Buy-Sell Event. Upon the occurrence of a Buy-Sell Event, the affected member or the executor, administrator or other legal representative in the event of death or declaration of legal incompetency of that member will give notice of the Buy-Sell Event to the Company. If the affected member or its representative fails to give such notice within ten days of the occurrence of the Buy-Sell Event, then any other member may give the notice to the Company at any time.

8.3 Company's Purchase Option. Upon the occurrence of a Buy-Sell Event, the Company may purchase the affected member's membership interests by providing the affected member or its representative notice of the Company's intention to purchase within thirty days of the Company receiving notice of the Buy-Sell Event. The Company may purchase the member's membership interests at the purchase price agreed upon by the parties or an independent appraiser selected by the parties. If the parties cannot agree upon an independent appraiser, each party will appoint one appraiser, with those two appraisers selecting a third appraiser to resolve any valuation disputes. Once the purchase price is determined by the parties or the appraisers, as the case may be, the Company will close the purchase of the affected member's membership interests within sixty days of that determination.

Name:

Proposed Revisions to Operating Agreement

Privileged & Confidential
For Discussion Purposes Only

ARTICLE II - MANAGEMENT

ARTICLE VI - TRANSFER OF MEMBERSHIP INTERESTS

Proposed Revisions to Operating Agreement, continued

ARTICLE VII - BUY-SELL

CHAPTER FOUR

Process of Incorporation
Starting the Start-Up

YOU JUST JOINED a small law firm that focuses on business law. The firm is well-respected in the business community and it frequently helps entrepreneurs with entity formation and financing issues. Many of these companies operate in the technology and biotechnology industries and are attractive investment opportunities for venture capital firms. In fact, many of the entrepreneurs are referred to the law firm by venture capital firms.

On your second day at your new job, one of the partners walks into your office and hands you a file. The file contains a few letters, some handwritten notes and a business plan. The partner explains that Rachel Lock and Ted Strong recently hired the law firm to help them launch a new business. Both Lock and Strong hold graduate certificates in Cyber Security. They have become experts in the field and have been working for the past several years for a Fortune 100 company. They are tired of "giving up" their innovations in cyber-security technology to the company and have decided to start their own cyber-security business.

The partner explains that Lock and Strong have been in discussions with their employer regarding an amicable termination agreement that will reduce the restrictions imposed on them by their current nondisclosure agreements and noncompete covenants with the company. The partner is optimistic that those discussions will wrap up shortly with a positive result that will allow Lock and Strong to start their own company while providing their soon-to-be-former employer access to the new company's products and services on fair and reasonable terms. In fact, the partner proudly proclaims that she helped facilitate this compromise by highlighting the cost reductions that the employer might achieve through outsourcing its cyber-security needs. This outsourcing platform is a central component of Lock's and Strong's business plan.

Unsure of your role in this new matter, you ask the partner how you can help. The partner explains that Lock and Strong want to be ready to go with their new company as soon as the agreement is in place with their employer. Accordingly, the partner needs you to: (i) draft the new company's articles/certificate of incorporation (check the law in your jurisdiction to determine if you should use "articles of incorporation" or "certificate of incorporation"); and (ii) create a checklist for the clients of other necessary or recommended steps that will help the company get off to a great start (e.g., drafting bylaws, identifying directors and officers, etc.). You are excited to have this drafting opportunity so early in your career at the law firm and are determined to do an outstanding job. You get right to work.

You review the file again and notice the following information in the handwritten notes from the partner:

Checklist of Steps for Lock and Strong

- ▶ Clients still kicking around company name, but seem settled on Lock-Strong Security

- ▶ Clients will be incorporators and founders

- ▶ 10,000,000 authorized common stock—6,000,000 to founders with each investing $3,000 to start

- ▶ 5,000,000 authorized preferred stock (do not contemplate needing immediately but likely will need for future financing flexibility)

▶ Five member board; Lock and Strong want say in board and company management

▶ Lock and Strong will be CEO and COO, respectively; contemplate small number of employees initially

▶ Want to enter into service contract with employer as soon as possible to lock employer into terms and have at least one client from the start

▶ Want liability protection

Using the information from the client file, prepare a draft of the articles/certificate of incorporation for Lock-Strong Security. Your firm prefers the format that is reproduced at the end of Chapter Four. In addition, complete the firm's Start-Up Company Checklist that follows the articles/certificate of incorporation form.

 Points to Consider:

1. Which items in the partner's notes must be included in the articles/certificate of incorporation?

2. Can you include her other points in the articles/certificate of incorporation, even if not required by state law? If so, is there a disadvantage to including everything?

3. Who decides what goes in the articles/certificate of incorporation and what goes in the bylaws or other governance documents—you or the client?

• DRAFTING A CERTIFICATE OF INCORPORATION

Name:

STATE *of* [_____]
[_____] *of* INCORPORATION
A STOCK CORPORATION

ARTICLE I
Name

_____

_____

_____

_____

ARTICLE II
Purpose

_____

_____

_____

_____

_____

_____

_____

_____

_____

_____

ARTICLE III

[_____]

_____
_____
_____
_____

_____

_____

ARTICLE IV

[_____]

_____
_____
_____
_____
_____
_____
_____
_____

ARTICLE V

[_____]

_____
_____
_____
_____
_____
_____
_____

• DRAFTING A CERTIFICATE OF INCORPORATION

ARTICLE VI

[————————————————————]

_____

_____

_____

_____

_____

_____

ARTICLE VII

[————————————————————]

_____

_____

_____

_____

_____

_____

_____

_____

ARTICLE VIII

[————————————————————]

_____

_____

_____

_____

_____

_____

_____

_____

• DRAFTING A CERTIFICATE OF INCORPORATION

Name:

Attorney-Client Privileged
Attorneys' Work Product

Start-Up Company Checklist

▶

▶

▶

▶

▶

▶

CHAPTER FIVE

Breach of Fiduciary Duty: Duty of Care
Hindsight Is Twenty-Twenty

PAULA LEADER IS THE CEO of one of your law firm's good clients, For the Love of Reading ("FLR"). FLR owns a chain of retail book and magazine stores. It is incorporated in Delaware and has its headquarters in Lincoln, Nebraska. FLR does business throughout the United States. Paula is clearly upset when she enters your office. When you ask Paula what is the matter, she places a Complaint filed against FLR on your desk and responds with the following explanation.

Sam Steamer is a disgruntled shareholder of FLR. Sam has owned FLR stock for the past twenty years. He has generally been very supportive of FLR's board of directors, but recently he has been making noise that the board is incompetent and mismanaging the company. Knowing both the members of the board and their qualifi- cations, you are somewhat surprised by the allegations in the Complaint. You ask Paula for more details on Sam's perspective.

Apparently, Sam has been upset with FLR's recent lackluster performance and the corresponding drop in stock price. He attributes FLR's disappointing results to the refusal of FLR's board of directors to include a coffee café in each retail store. According to Sam's Complaint, research in the industry clearly shows that people prefer to shop at bookstores that also offer the aroma of fresh-brewed coffee. The Complaint also alleges that historical financial data of FLR's competitors show a significant increase in book sales when they redesigned their business models to include a coffee café. The Complaint further alleges that the board's refusal to offer coffee at FLR's retail stores stems solely from the board's "old-fashioned" notions regarding the ambiance of a neighborhood bookstore that underlies FLR's original business plan.

You know from prior discussions with Paula and FLR's board that the board is in fact against incorporating coffee cafés into the retail stores, but for some good reasons. FLR's board believes that coffee cafés do not increase book and magazine sales. In fact, reports presented to the board by its professional advisors suggest that cafés may result in lower sales because people avoid buying books and magazines that have been "previewed" by others while drinking their coffee. These same reports also suggest that people previewing books and magazines in cafés rarely buy these items and take them home. Based on these reports, the board in the past has unanimously rejected proposals to add coffee cafés to FLR's business model.

After explaining the story, Paula seeks your advice regarding the litigation commenced against FLR by Sam. You tell Paula that you will review the Complaint and provide her with a preliminary assessment as soon as possible. She is very grateful for your prompt attention to this matter and asks you to go ahead and start drafting whatever legal documents might be necessary so that you can discuss everything at one meeting. You agree to do so and indicate that you will call her in a few days with an update.

Upon reviewing the Complaint, you decide to prepare a draft of the major points to include in the Motion to Dismiss Complaint first, which you suspect Paula will want to file immediately. Although there is a lot of background and, from your perspective, irrelevant information in the Complaint, the Complaint asserts the following two causes of action against the board of directors:

Count I: Breach of Fiduciary Duty: Duty of Care

81. Plaintiff realleges paragraphs 1-80 as if fully set forth herein.

82. Each Defendant, as a member of the Company's Board of Directors, breached her or his fiduciary duties to the Company by, among other things, failing to exercise due care in developing and managing the Company's business and operational plans. Specifically, the Defendants have caused significant economic and reputational harm to the Company through their failure to incorporate into the Company's retail stores a space for patrons to relax, review and consider purchases of the Company's products and enjoy beverages and snacks. The Defendants have acted recklessly in these decisions to the direct detriment of the Company and its shareholders.

83. By reason of the foregoing, the Company has been damaged in an amount to be determined at trial.

Count II: Breach of Fiduciary Duty: Duty of Good Faith

84. Plaintiff realleges paragraphs 1-83 as if fully set forth herein.

85. Each Defendant, as a member of the Company's Board of Directors, breached her or his fiduciary duties to the Company by, among other things, failing to act in good faith in developing and managing the Company's business and operational plans. Specifically, the Defendants have caused significant economic and reputational harm to the Company through their failure to incorporate into the Company's retail stores a space for patrons to relax, review and consider purchases of the Company's products and enjoy beverages and snacks. In making these decisions, the Defendants have intentionally ignored a known duty to act in the best interests of the Company. Instead, the Directors have continued to pursue a flawed and outdated business plan to the direct detriment of the Company and its shareholders.

86. By reason of the foregoing, the Company has been damaged in an amount to be determined at trial.

Before starting your draft, you pull out FLR's governance documents and take a quick look at FLR's Certificate of Incorporation. You notice that the Certificate of Incorporation has never been amended and make a note to discuss with the company whether it needs to be updated once this current crisis passes. You then begin to draft the Motion to Dismiss Complaint. The Motion will be accompanied by a more detailed Memorandum in Support of Defendants' Motion to Dismiss Complaint, but you decide to leave that document for a later date. Your hope is to outline your arguments and your discussion with Paula in a concise Motion.

Review the Certificate of Incorporation for FLR, which is reproduced at the end of Chapter Five. Next, outline the major points you will address in the Defendants' Motion to Dismiss Complaint that follows the Certificate of Incorporation.

 Points to Consider:

1. Has the plaintiff alleged sufficient facts to support its causes of action against the defendants? How would you characterize the core nature of those causes of action? Does that help you formulate a defense?

2. Does the Certificate of Incorporation provide an ironclad defense for the directors? How do you advise the directors on this point?

3. Can you file the Motion to Dismiss Complaint on behalf of the directors, or does your relationship with the company preclude that?

$$\text{State of Delaware}$$
Certificate of Incorporation
A Stock Corporation

ARTICLE I
Name

The name of the corporation is **For the Love of Reading, Inc.** (the "Corporation").

ARTICLE II
Purpose

The purpose for which the Corporation is organized is to conduct any and all lawful business for which corporations can be organized under the General Corporation Law of the State of Delaware.

ARTICLE III
Powers

The Corporation has the power to engage in any lawful activity under the General Corporation Law of the State of Delaware.

ARTICLE IV
Registered Agent

The Corporation's registered agent is The Trust Company, and its registered office in the State of Delaware is located at One Main Street, Wilmington, Delaware.

ARTICLE V
Authorized Shares

The Corporation is authorized to issue one billion shares of common stock with a par value of $.0001.

ARTICLE VI
Directors and Officers

6.1 The Corporation's initial Board of Directors shall be comprised of the following persons:

John Smith, Chairman and Chief Executive Officer
Barbara Low, Director
Nicholas Bloom, Director

6.2 The business and affairs of the Corporation shall be managed by or under the direction of its Board of Directors.

6.3 The number of directors constituting the Board of Directors shall not be less than three nor more than nine, as authorized from time to time by a vote of a majority of the Board of Directors.

ARTICLE VII
Bylaws

The Incorporator shall adopt the initial bylaws of the Corporation. The stockholders may amend the bylaws at any time by the provisions therein.

ARTICLE VIII
Indemnification and Limited Liability

8.1 Directors, officers, employees and agents of the Corporation may be indemnified by the Corporation to such extent as is permitted by the laws of the State of Delaware.

8.2 A director of the Corporation shall not be personally liable to the Corporation or its stockholders for monetary damages for breach of fiduciary duty as a director to the fullest extent permitted by the General Corporation Law of Delaware, as the same now exists or as hereafter amended.

ARTICLE IX
Dissolution

Upon dissolution, assets shall be distributed by the Board of Directors according to the applicable state statute. Further provisions regarding distribution upon dissolution shall be stated in the Corporation's bylaws.

ARTICLE X
Amendment of Certificate of Incorporation

The Corporation reserves the right to amend, alter, change or repeal any provision of this Certificate of Incorporation as provided under the General Corporation Law of Delaware, as the same now exists or as hereafter amended, and all rights conferred on stockholders therein granted are subject to this reservation.

ARTICLE XI
Incorporator

The name and mailing address of the Incorporator are as follows:

John Smith
L Street
Lincoln, Nebraska

I, John Smith, for the purpose of forming a corporation under the laws of the State of Delaware, do make, file and record this Certificate, and do certify that the facts herein stated are true, and I have accordingly hereunto set my hand this

20th day of June, 1991.

John Smith
_____
BY: John Smith, Incorporator

Name:

Defendants' Motion To Dismiss Complaint

Pursuant to [insert applicable rules], the above-captioned Defendants hereby move to dismiss the Plaintiff's Complaint. The Defendants' Motion to Dismiss Complaint should be granted for the following reasons:

1.

2.

3.

Defendants' Motion To Dismiss Complaint, continued

4.

In further support of this Motion, the Defendants submit the accompanying Memorandum in Support of Defendants' Motion to Dismiss Complaint.

WHEREFORE, for the reasons set forth above and in their supporting Memorandum, the Defendants respectfully request that this Court enter an order dismissing the Plaintiff's Complaint with prejudice and grant such other relief as is just and reasonable.

Interested Director Transactions
But It's a Win-Win Transaction

JANE REIT IS A WELL-RESPECTED real estate developer who
develops, sells and manages commercial real estate throughout the
United States. She is known for being a hard, but fair, negotiator. She
is incredibly knowledgeable about not only the commercial real estate
market but also about many of the companies (and their respective
industries) that buy or lease her properties.

Jane's extensive experience and industry knowledge, as well
as her general business sense, make her an attractive candidate for
many companies' boards of directors. Jane enjoys serving on boards
of directors, but she will only serve on the boards of two or three
companies at any given time because of the time commitment
associated with board service. Jane takes her board service very
seriously, and for this reason she is generally regarded as a productive
and valued board member.

You met Jane through your representation of Fashion Store, Inc.
Jane is a member of Fashion Store's board of directors. You have been
Fashion Store's outside legal counsel for more years than you care to
count. Over the years, you have become good friends with many of
Fashion Store's directors and officers, including Jane. In fact, you and
Jane bonded almost immediately upon discovering that you graduated

from the same university and both remain diehard fans of the school's top-ranked basketball team. Jane has even invited you to sit in her luxury suite during some of the school's home basketball games.

Fashion Store owns and operates a chain of retail clothing stores. Its business model typically involves locating old (sometimes abandoned) warehouses and buying the land and buildings at bargain prices. Fashion Store then converts the warehouse into a trendy, freestanding retail store. Its retail stores also typically attract other retailers, restaurants and hotels to the area, which can provide a much-needed economic boost to the local community.

Jane's expertise has been incredibly valuable to Fashion Store's board and management team. You have even picked up some real estate strategies from her along the way. Jane also is a nice fit on Fashion Store's board because she generally does not pursue real estate transactions in the same geographical areas as Fashion Store, and Fashion Store owns, rather than leases, its store locations. (Note: Jane and Fashion Store are not in any landlord-tenant relationships.) In fact, Jane's professional endeavors and her service on Fashion Store's board have never presented a conflict of interest or even the appearance of impropriety.

Consequently, the following e-mail takes you somewhat by surprise:

To: lawyer@lawfirm.com
From: Jane Reit
Subject: Potential Acquisition/Privileged and Confidential

How about that game last night? Can you believe we pulled it out? I am still in awe over the win!

But we can talk basketball later—I need your help on something. I have an industrial park in my portfolio that is really struggling to survive. The Fortune 500 company that occupied three of the five buildings in the park picked up and moved its headquarters to another state. Now I have two empty office buildings and one huge empty warehouse. I know that it is not the typical Fashion Store location, but I think it would be a good market expansion for Fashion Store. And—between us—it would really help me out because I could get rid of the warehouse (which no one wants but I know Fashion Store can afford to take at market price) and use Fashion Store's arrival to attract new tenants for the other two buildings. We might even be able to get a restaurant or two to move into the area. It will be a win-win for everyone. I plan to propose the deal at the board meeting next week.

You sit there for a moment just staring at the e-mail. The euphoria you had from the big basketball win has vanished. The e-mail requires a response. You are counsel to Fashion Store, and you now have information that likely is material to Fashion Store but appears to be conveyed with some expectation of confidentiality. There are problems with the proposed transaction itself as well. After getting a cup of coffee, you sit down to draft an e-mail in response.

Points to Consider:

1. What are Jane's duties to Fashion Store? Does her proposed course of action run afoul of those duties?

2. Is there any way that Jane can propose, and Fashion Store can pursue, the stated course of action?

3. Who is your client? What are your duties to your client? Do those duties require you to take any affirmative action here?

Draft E-mail Response

To: Jane Reit

Cc:

From:

Subject:

Jane:

I am in receipt of your e-mail with the subject line
"Potential Acquisition/Privileged and Confidential."

CHAPTER SEVEN

Derivative Litigation and the Demand Letter

They Will Not Sue Themselves

MEGA, INC. is a large telecommunications provider. Mega is incorporated in a state that follows the Model Business Corporation Act and is a publicly-held company, with its stock listed on NASDAQ. Its stock price has increased substantially in the past seven years because of very lucrative government contracts obtained with the United States and several foreign countries.

Unfortunately for Mega, its good fortunes overseas were not the result of its products or services, but rather were the result of several illegal payments to top-ranking government officials in various foreign countries. A recent press release by the Securities and Exchange Commission tells at least part of the story:

FOR IMMEDIATE RELEASE
2012-509

SEC Charges Mega, Inc. for International Bribery

WASHINGTON, D.C.—The Securities and Exchange Commission today charged Mega, Inc. with bribing foreign officials in order to secure lucrative telecommunications services contracts. In a Complaint filed in federal court in Washington, D.C., the SEC alleges that at least three members of Mega's board of directors were involved in the design and implementation of a bribery scheme in violation of the U.S. Foreign Corrupt Practices Act. According to the Complaint, the bribery scheme began several years ago and the payments were filtered through shell entities organized under the laws of the various foreign jurisdictions...

The vast majority of Mega's board of directors was shocked and horrified by the news. Speculation about the three board members identified in the press release—Kathy, Brian and Richard—ran rampant. A few board members even commented on the coincidental timing between the illegal payments and Kathy, Brian and Richard each purchasing luxurious vacation homes and yachts.

Kathy, Brian and Richard are members of the board's three-person Compliance Committee. The Compliance Committee meets regularly with Mega's Chief Compliance Officer, and it is responsible for, among other things, reviewing the implementation and effectiveness of the company's compliance program. The Compliance Committee was created approximately ten years ago after a two-year internal investigation to monitor Mega's compliance with domestic and foreign laws and to provide a contact point for Mega's employees to report suspected violations of applicable law. Only six of the seventeen current board members were on Mega's board at the time the board created the Compliance Committee, and three of those six members are Kathy, Brian and Richard.

Under its charter, the Compliance Committee does not have any authority to act on behalf of the company or to decide substantive matters. Rather, the Compliance Committee's role is limited to monitoring and reporting on compliance issues. The board worked with the Compliance Committee to draft a detailed employee handbook that explains Mega's compliance program and the consequences of failing to comply or report noncompliance. Every Mega employee receives a copy of the handbook. The Compliance Committee provides semi-annual reports to the board, and these reports have never indicated problems, or even suspected problems, with Mega's legal compliance.

Although the rumors concerning the three members of the Compliance Committee are troubling, the board's immediate problem is a significant drop in Mega's stock price.

Since the issuance of the SEC's press release, the board and management team have been overwhelmed by investors' inquiries, the market reaction generally and the SEC investigation process. Now, you are about to make things even more challenging for the board.

Three of Mega's shareholders recently retained your law firm. The shareholders want to hold the board accountable for failing to monitor properly Mega's employees and prevent the illegal payment scheme. You have reviewed the common challenges to shareholder derivative litigation with your clients (i.e., the three Mega shareholders). Notwithstanding the difficult legal obstacles presented, the Mega shareholders are determined and want to press forward with litigation against the Mega board of directors. (Note: The Mega shareholders have asked for a contingent fee arrangement, which firm management is considering. You have been instructed to move forward on the matter pending these discussions.)

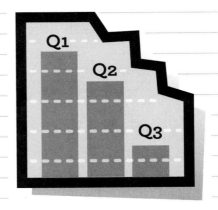

Due diligence efforts so far have uncovered the press release, Mega's Compliance Committee charter and a copy of Mega's compliance program and related employee handbook. Based on the description of these materials in the fact pattern, prepare a letter on behalf of the Mega shareholders using the Demand Letter reproduced at the end of Chapter Seven. In preparing the Demand Letter, consider who should be named as defendants in any potential lawsuit, the causes of action to be asserted against those defendants and the facts supporting the causes of action. In addition, be sure to state what you want Mega's board of directors to do with the information you are providing.

 Points to Consider:

1. Who are the potential defendants in your lawsuit? Do you sue only members of the board who were involved in creating or serving on the compliance committee or, perhaps, only members of the current board of directors? Is there a benefit to just naming everyone as a defendant?

2. What elements need to be contained as part of your demand letter?

3. Can you write your demand letter based on the shareholders' allegations and recitation of the facts, or do you first need to do something more?

Demand Letter

Small, Tuff & Winn, LLC
New York, Philadelphia, Wilmington

[Date]

Board of Directors
Attn: Chairperson of the Board
Mega, Inc.
1000 Corporate Lane
City, State 00000

Re: <u>Demand to File Litigation Against Directors of Mega, Inc.</u>

Dear Madam Chairperson:

I represent three shareholders of Mega, Inc., and I am writing in respect of the fraud, mismanagement and illegal conduct disclosed in the recent press release of the U.S. Securities and Exchange Commission. This letter details the identity of the wrongdoers, their detrimental conduct and the resulting injury to Mega and its shareholders. On behalf of the shareholders identified in this letter, I respectfully request and demand that the Board of Directors immediately authorize the company to file a lawsuit against the wrongdoers seeking, among other things, monetary damages and all other appropriate relief under applicable law.

(continued on next page)

Demand Letter, continued

I. Identity of Wrongdoers

II. Detrimental Conduct

III. Causes of Action

Demand Letter, continued

IV. Harm to Mega

I further certify that each shareholder identified below my signature block purchased their shares of Mega stock more than 15 years ago, collectively own more than 5% of the stock and adequately represent the interests of all Mega's shareholders. Indeed, my clients seek to have the company pursue and hold the wrongdoers liable for their detrimental conduct in a manner that benefits the company and all of its shareholders.

Sincerely,

CHAPTER EIGHT

Indemnification Provisions
Pigs Get Fat, Hogs Get Slaughtered

ONE OF YOUR FAVORITE CLIENTS is an eccentric individual who has made a well-deserved name for herself in the biomedical industry. Dr. Martha Green is a scientist by training, but she possesses innate business skills, which she honed by earning an MBA at a nationally recognized business school. Her unique skill set has helped her move beyond the laboratory to the marketing and profit-creation side of the industry. She is best known for her ability to create private-public partnerships between private-sector biomedical companies and top-notch university research departments, which often streamlines and accelerates the research-to-market process.

Dr. Green has a very impressive track record and career path. Starting out in academia, she quickly moved up the ranks at her university from a Professor of Biomedical Sciences to Associate Dean of Research. She then accepted the challenge of running her university's Office of Research and Development. Dr. Green used that platform to promote the value of private-public partnerships, creating a number of very profitable ventures for her university. Dr. Green eventually left academia and held a high-ranking position at the United States Food and Drug Administration's ("FDA") Center for Biologics Evaluation and Research. Although she enjoyed her time with the FDA, Dr. Green is not one to stay in any one position too long. Ready for a new challenge, she left her government position, and she has been writing a book and lecturing around the country. Dr. Green's next big challenge to pursue other opportunities has ended up on your desk.

A large pharmaceutical company is pursuing Dr. Green to serve as the company's Chief Innovation Officer. Dr. Green is intrigued by the opportunity. The position would give her significant control over the company's research and development initiatives and allow her to pursue her passion for private-public partnerships from the other side of the equation—the private-sector side. The gleam in her eyes suggests that she is excited about this new opportunity. Yet, you also detect some hint of reservation as she describes the company's situation.

As you talk through this opportunity with Dr. Green, her concerns become more apparent. The pharmaceutical company is a publicly traded company. Although she believes in the company's mission, its management team has been subject to several large, high-profile lawsuits in the past. These lawsuits range from patent disputes to products liability claims to shareholder class-action lawsuits. Dr. Green is unwilling to risk her family's financial security by personally incurring high legal defense costs.

Dr. Green explains that she has raised her concerns with the company's Chief Executive Officer, who has assured her that the company "takes care of its own." He gave her a copy of the company's certificate of incorporation, which reads:

V. Limitation of Liability

To the full extent permitted by state law, no director or officer of the company made a party to a proceeding in that capacity shall be liable to the Company or its shareholders for any monetary damages incurred in connection with such proceeding.

VI. Indemnification

To the full extent permitted by state law, the Company shall indemnify any director or officer made a party to a proceeding in that capacity against any liability incurred by such director or officer in connection with such proceeding.

After reading these provisions, you share Dr. Green's concerns. You propose that she request an indemnification agreement from the company. Dr. Green likes the idea of having a separate indemnification agreement with the company. She also would like some guidance regarding what aspects of the proposed agreement she absolutely needs, and what aspects she safely could live without. She understands the give-and-take dynamics of negotiation, but would like a better sense of the legal context to frame her negotiation strategy with the company. You assure Dr. Green that you understand the task at hand and that you will get to work on it immediately.

Using the Indemnification Agreement reproduced at the end of Chapter Eight, prepare a proposed agreement for Dr. Green to present to the company. In preparing the Indemnification Agreement, try to anticipate how the company may respond or counter your proposed terms.

 Points to Consider:

1. Under what circumstances might Dr. Green incur monetary expenses or damages as a result of her new position with the company? Are any of those circumstances covered by the existing provisions of the certificate of incorporation?

2. What additional coverage can you provide for Dr. Green under applicable state law? Would you advise Dr. Green to also request information concerning the company's director and officer liability coverage?

3. What would you advise Dr. Green regarding her negotiation strategy? What points are the most important for her financial protection?

Indemnification Agreement

Name:

BIG PHARMACEUTICAL COMPANY
INDEMNIFICATION AGREEMENT
CHIEF INNOVATION OFFICER

THIS INDEMNIFICATION AGREEMENT ("Agreement") is made as of the _____ day of _____, 20 _____, by and between Big Pharmaceutical Company, a [State] corporation (the "Company"), and Dr. Martha Green, as Chief Innovation Officer of the Company (the "CIO").

   WHEREAS, the CIO is an officer of the Company and provides valuable services to the Company; and

   WHEREAS, the Company's Bylaws (the "Bylaws") provide for the indemnification of the directors and executive officers of the Company; and

   WHEREAS, the Bylaws and applicable state law permit the Company to enter into indemnification agreements with its officers and directors; and

   WHEREAS, the CIO desires, and the Company agrees to provide, additional assurances and protection against liability that she may incur in her capacity as CIO of the Company; and

   WHEREAS, the CIO and the Company have agreed to enter into this Agreement.

Indemnifaction Agreement, continued

        NOW, THEREFORE, in consideration of the foregoing and the CIO's service as an officer of the Company, the parties agree as follows:

1. Indemnification.

2. Expenses.

3. Notice.

Indemnifaction Agreement, continued

4. Enforcement.

5. Insurance Coverage.

6. Miscellaneous.

CHAPTER NINE

M&A and Board Resolutions
To Sell or Not to Sell, That Is the Question

STEVE ROTARY IS THE CHIEF EXECUTIVE OFFICER of Family Electronics Corp. ("FEC"). FEC is incorporated in Delaware, and its stock is publicly traded on the New York Stock Exchange ("NYSE"). Rotary believes in running a tight ship. He maintains control over the company's day-to-day operations. He also has significant influence over the selection of individuals hired by the company for its management team, as well as those asked to serve on the company's board of directors. FEC's fifteen-member board consists of eleven outside directors (who qualify as "independent directors" under NYSE's listing standards), Rotary, FEC's Chief Financial Officer and two other executives.

Despite Rotary's best efforts, FEC is losing money and market share. Its core business—selling phones, radios, televisions and gaming consoles for the entire family—is facing stiff competition from volume discount retailers and online distributors. Rotary believes that FEC's poor performance is temporary and that cheap products and online shopping will soon lose their novelty. Accordingly, Rotary is maintaining FEC's focus on its current advertising campaign and traditional business model, which offers customers a home simulation shopping experience.

Rotary likes to hedge his bets, however, and also has a "Plan B" just in case "that online shopping thing really catches on." He is negotiating a deal to sell FEC to Electronics for Less ("E-Less"), a leading online electronics distributor. E-Less is owned by a private equity firm that would like to use FEC's customer list for its online business and then sell the real estate on which FEC's stores are located. The following letter is the latest correspondence on this potential deal:

Dear Steve:

I enjoyed meeting with you again today. As we discussed, Electronics for Less is willing to purchase substantially all of Family Electronic Corp.'s assets for a small premium on the market valuation of the assets, subject to our due diligence and the final appraisal of the assets. E-Less will not assume any of FEC's liabilities and will be under no obligation to continue any of FEC's contracts, including any employment contracts. We understand that this transaction is subject to the approval of FEC's board of directors, as well as any necessary regulatory approvals. The transaction also will be subject to representations, warranties, covenants and conditions as customary in the industry. We anticipate sending you a non-binding term sheet by the end of the week.

Sincerely,

Harriet

At the most recent board meeting, Rotary reported FEC's continued losses and its plan to continue the expansion efforts. The meeting lasted over four hours as board members questioned Rotary's research and reasoning. Rotary responded to the board's questions in a satisfactory manner, but never mentioned his discussions with E-Less. Likewise, in FEC's press release, which was approved at the board meeting and issued the following day, only FEC's poor financial results and ongoing expansion plans were reported. Rotary voted in favor of approving the press release, which accurately reflected the board's discussion of these issues. FEC's stock price dropped dramatically on issuance of the press release—from $25 per share to around $15 per share.

Rotary was quietly pleased by the stock price decline and purchased a significant portion of FEC's stock on the open market. FEC's banks, however, were not so pleased by the sharp drop, which triggered a default under FEC's loan agreements. The banks announced that they would stop funding FEC's expansion plans. Following the banks' announcement, E-Less announced its intention to buy FEC. The lawyers for FEC and E-Less hammered out the details of the deal, which were presented to the boards of both companies. Outside legal counsel to FEC has been representing the company in the negotiations and documentation of the contemplated transaction.

FEC's board of directors has hired you to represent and advise the board in this transaction. Although the board has tremendous respect for the company's outside legal counsel, the directors believe that the additional expense and potential delay associated with bringing in separate counsel is worth costs given the "bet the company" nature of the proposed transaction. Based on your preliminary due diligence, you have several questions and concerns to discuss with the board. Your immediate task, however, is to prepare resolutions for the board of directors in the event the directors approve the transaction.

Draft the Board Resolutions for FEC's board of directors to adopt in the event the directors decide to approve the proposed purchase of FEC by E-Less. The Board Resolutions are reproduced at the end of Chapter Nine. In addition, write a list of potential questions and related issues that you will review with the board members in providing legal advice concerning the board's due diligence obligations.

 Points to Consider:

1. What type of information should be included in the board resolutions? What is the purpose of the resolutions?

2. Should your concerns regarding the transaction impact how you draft the board resolutions? Should they impact the board's decision?

3. What if any conversations should you have with the company's counsel regarding the proposed transaction? Do you agree with the board's decision to hire separate counsel?

Name:

Board Resolution Form

RESOLUTIONS OF BOARD OF DIRECTORS
Family Electronics Corp.

Resolutions Approving Transaction

WHEREAS, the Board of Directors (the "Board") of Family Electronics Corp. (the "Company") held a meeting on [date] to discuss the sale of substantially all of the Company's assets to Electronics for Less ("E-Less"); and

WHEREAS,

WHEREAS,

NOW THEREFORE LET IT BE:

RESOLVED,

Board Resolution, continued

RESOLVED,

RESOLVED,

RESOLVED,

RESOLVED,

RESOLVED,

Name:

Attorney-Client Privileged
Attorneys' Work Product

Due Diligence Questions for Board/Company Representatives

I. Events Leading Up to Proposed Transaction

II. Negotiation and Terms of Proposed Transaction

III. Board Consideration and Approval of Proposed Transaction

CHAPTER TEN

Voting Agreements and Representations
One for All and All for One

NICK BLOCK IS A SHAREHOLDER of Everyday Runners, Inc., a national retail chain that sells sports gear and clothing for the entire family. Block owns 10% of the company. The other major shareholders include: the founder of the company and her family members, who collectively own 25% of the company; Cynthia Stack, who owns 12%; and Jeremy Light, who owns 8%. The company's remaining shares are widely distributed among employees and other investors.

Everyday Runners has a nine-member board of directors. The directors are elected on a staggered basis, with three director positions to be elected each year at the company's annual meeting. The company also adheres to a plurality voting scheme for the election of directors. The relevant provisions of the bylaws read:

VII. Board of Directors

A. <u>Number</u>

The number of directors that will constitute the board will be no less than 3 and no more than 25, as determined by the board of directors or the shareholders.

B. Election

The directors will be elected by a plurality of the votes of the shares present in person or represented by proxy at the annual meeting and entitled to vote on the election of directors.

C. Term of Board

The board of directors will be divided into three classes as nearly equal in number as possible, designated Class I, Class II and Class III. Each class of directors will serve for a term ending on the date of the third annual meeting following the election of that class; provided, however, that the initial term for Class I will end on the date of the first annual meeting following the initial election of that class and the initial term for Class II will end on the date of the second annual meeting following the initial election of that class.

Block has come to see one of the corporate partners at your firm regarding the governance structure of Everyday Runners. The partner invites you to sit in on the meeting, which invitation you enthusiastically accept as it likely means you will get to work on this new matter. Block explains that the company's approach to the election and composition of the board of directors is a vestige of when the founder retained greater control over the company. He notes that, although she is still a major shareholder, the founder has cashed out a significant portion of her equity in the company and has "checked out" of the management of the company. As a result, Block is concerned that the company lacks leadership. He believes it is time to take the company in a new direction.

Everyday Runners has been in the news lately, generating headlines like the following:

The financial media likewise has been touting the company's ability to capitalize on the family fitness craze while down-sizing its brick and mortar stores, enhancing its online offerings to meet the needs of its loyal customer base and building up a large cash reserve (even calling the company a "cash cow").

Family Fitness:
The Family that Runs Together Stays Together

The employees of Everyday Runners are practicing what they preach at the company's annual Family Fun 1K run.

As the meeting continues, Block explains that the company's dispersed ownership, the founder's control over 25% of the stock and the plurality voting scheme have created the perfect storm—the company's proposed slate of directors is always approved, with the same directors, the same management team and the same conservative management style prevailing. Block wants change; he wants to unlock the company's true value.

Block notes that he has spoken with Stack and Light about these issues, and they agree with his position. The three also have agreed in principle to pool their votes. Block comments that the three are of "like mind" concerning the election of directors and potential transactions that the company might pursue. Before the corporate partner can react, Block says he understands that pooling their votes does not change the slate of directors proposed by the company or solve the problems potentially posed by the classified board structure. He points to those issues as part of the reason for his visit.

The meeting continues for a little longer but nothing else of much substance is discussed. After the meeting, the corporate partner says that he needs two things from you:

First, he wants you to draft a simple voting agreement to be executed among Block, Stack and Light. The voting agreement should only address voting on director elections and material transactions and contain standard provisions to ensure that the parties can live up to, and enforce, the terms of their bargain.

Second, he wants you to summarize in one paragraph the steps necessary for Block to change the terms of the bylaws, specifically those concerning the classified structure of the board and plurality voting. Although the corporate partner wants to give it more thought, he thinks that annual elections and cumulative voting might be a better governance structure. He emphasizes that the summary of the amendment process should be an "executive summary"—concise and easily understood by the client.

You head back to your office and begin reviewing the file. A letter in the file from Everyday Runners to one of your favorite professional athletes catches your attention. The letter asks the athlete to become a spokesperson for the company. At the top of the letter, you discover a handwritten note.

You can't believe that you are working on a deal that puts you just a few degrees removed from your favorite athlete. After a quick telephone call to your best friend (in which you brag all about this new representation), you focus on the matter at hand.

Nick—

Can you please talk to this guy? I think we can get him on board if we show him a little love.

Following the instructions provided by the partner, draft the key provisions of the Shareholder Voting Agreement reproduced at the end of Chapter Ten. After drafting the Shareholder Voting Agreement, prepare the executive summary requested by the partner.

 Points to Consider:

1. Does a voting agreement help Block here? If so, how? What matters should be covered by the voting agreement?

2. What provisions of the bylaws might Block want to change? Why?

3. You start to regret calling your best friend and telling him about this new matter. Why might you now be concerned about that call?

Name:

Shareholder Voting Agreement

THIS AGREEMENT, is made by and among Nick Block ("Block"), Cynthia Stack ("Stack") and Jeremy Light ("Light" and collectively with Block and Stack, the "Shareholders"), and is effective as of _____ , 20____.

Recitals

A. The Shareholders each own shares of common stock in Everyday Runners, Inc. (the "Company").

B. The Shareholders desire to vote their shares of common stock in favor of certain resolutions and matters as described below.

NOW, THEREFORE, in consideration of the foregoing and the mutual covenants and promises contained herein, the parties agree:

1. <u>Representations Regarding Stock Ownership.</u>

2. <u>Voting on Selection of Board of Directors.</u>

Shareholder Voting Agreement, continued

3. <u>Voting on Material Transactions.</u>

4. <u>Termination.</u>

5. <u>Enforcement.</u>

6. <u>Miscellaneous.</u>

Name:

Memorandum

To: Nick Block
From:
Re: Executive Summary of Bylaw Amendment Process
Date:

Appendix A
Selected Provisions of the Model Rules of Professional Conduct

▶ RULE 1.0 Terminology

(a) "Belief" or *"believes"* denotes that the person involved actually supposed the fact in question to be true. A person's belief may be inferred from circumstances.

(b) "Confirmed in writing," when used in reference to the informed consent of a person, denotes informed consent that is given in writing by the person or a writing that a lawyer promptly transmits to the person confirming an oral informed consent. See paragraph (e) for the definition of "informed consent." If it is not feasible to obtain or transmit the writing at the time the person gives informed consent, then the lawyer must obtain or transmit it within a reasonable time thereafter.

(c) "Firm" or *"law firm"* denotes a lawyer or lawyers in a law partnership, professional corporation, sole proprietorship or other association authorized to practice law, or lawyers employed in a legal services organization or the legal department of a corporation or other organization.

(d) "Fraud" or *"fraudulent"* denotes conduct that is fraudulent under the substantive or procedural law of the applicable jurisdiction and has a purpose to deceive.

(e) "Informed consent" denotes the agreement by a person to a proposed course of conduct after the lawyer has communicated adequate information and explanation about the material risks of and reasonably available alternatives to the proposed course of conduct.

(f) "Knowingly," "known," or *"knows"* denotes actual knowledge of the fact in question. A person's knowledge may be inferred from circumstances.

(g) "Partner" denotes a member of a partnership, a shareholder in a law firm organized as a professional corporation, or a member of an association authorized to practice law.

(h) *"Reasonable"* or *"reasonably"* when used in relation to conduct by a lawyer denotes the conduct of a reasonably prudent and competent lawyer.

(i) *"Reasonable belief"* or *"reasonably believes"* when used in reference to a lawyer denotes that the lawyer believes the matter in question and that the circumstances are such that the belief is reasonable.

(j) *"Reasonably should know"* when used in reference to a lawyer denotes that a lawyer of reasonable prudence and competence would ascertain the matter in question.

(k) *"Screened"* denotes the isolation of a lawyer from any participation in a matter through the timely imposition of procedures within a firm that are reasonably adequate under the circumstances to protect information that the isolated lawyer is obligated to protect under these Rules or other law.

(l) *"Substantial"* when used in reference to degree or extent denotes a material matter of clear and weighty importance.

(m) *"Tribunal"* denotes a court, an arbitrator in a binding arbitration proceeding or a legislative body, administrative agency or other body acting in an adjudicative capacity. A legislative body, administrative agency or other body acts in an adjudicative capacity when a neutral official, after the presentation of evidence or legal argument by a party or parties, will render a binding legal judgment directly affecting a party's interests in a particular matter.

(n) *"Writing"* or *"written"* denotes a tangible or electronic record of a communication or representation, including handwriting, typewriting, printing, photostating, photography, audio or video recording and e-mail. A writing includes an electronic sound, symbol or process attached to or logically associated with a writing and executed or adopted by a person with the intent to sign the writing.

▶ RULE 1.1 Competence

A lawyer shall provide competent representation to a client. Competent representation requires the legal knowledge, skill, thoroughness and preparation reasonably necessary for the representation.

▶ Rule 1.2 Scope of Representation and Allocation of Authority between Client and Lawyer

(a) Subject to paragraphs (c) and (d), a lawyer shall abide by a client's decisions concerning the objectives of representation and, as required by Rule 1.4, shall consult with the client as to the means by which they are to be pursued. A lawyer may take such action on behalf of the client as is impliedly authorized to carry out the representation. A lawyer shall abide by a client's decision whether to settle a matter. In a criminal case, the lawyer shall abide by the client's decision, after consultation with the lawyer, as to a plea to be entered, whether to waive jury trial and whether the client will testify.

(b) A lawyer's representation of a client, including representation by appointment, does not constitute an endorsement of the client's political, economic, social or moral views or activities.

(c) A lawyer may limit the scope of the representation if the limitation is reasonable under the circumstances and the client gives informed consent.

(d) A lawyer shall not counsel a client to engage, or assist a client, in conduct that the lawyer knows is criminal or fraudulent, but a lawyer may discuss the legal consequences of any proposed course of conduct with a client and may counsel or assist a client to make a good faith effort to determine the validity, scope, meaning or application of the law.

* * *

▶ RULE 1.4   Communication

(a) A lawyer shall:

(1) promptly inform the client of any decision or circumstance with respect to which the client's informed consent, as defined in Rule 1.0(e), is required by these Rules;

(2) reasonably consult with the client about the means by which the client's objectives are to be accomplished;

(3) keep the client reasonably informed about the status of the matter;

(4) promptly comply with reasonable requests for information; and

(5) consult with the client about any relevant limitation on the lawyer's conduct when the lawyer knows that the client expects assistance not permitted by the Rules of Professional Conduct or other law.

(b) A lawyer shall explain a matter to the extent reasonably necessary to permit the client to make informed decisions regarding the representation.

▶ RULE 1.5 Fees

(a) A lawyer shall not make an agreement for, charge, or collect an unreasonable fee or an unreasonable amount for expenses. The factors to be considered in determining the reasonableness of a fee include the following:

    (1) the time and labor required, the novelty and difficulty of the questions involved, and the skill requisite to perform the legal service properly;

    (2) the likelihood, if apparent to the client, that the acceptance of the particular employment will preclude other employment by the lawyer;

    (3) the fee customarily charged in the locality for similar legal services;

    (4) the amount involved and the results obtained;

    (5) the time limitations imposed by the client or by the circumstances;

    (6) the nature and length of the professional relationship with the client;

    (7) the experience, reputation, and ability of the lawyer or lawyers performing the services; and

    (8) whether the fee is fixed or contingent.

(b) The scope of the representation and the basis or rate of the fee and expenses for which the client will be responsible shall be communicated to the client, preferably in writing, before or within a reasonable time after commencing the representation, except when the lawyer will charge a regularly represented client on the same basis or rate. Any changes in the basis or rate of the fee or expenses shall also be communicated to the client.

(c) A fee may be contingent on the outcome of the matter for which the service is rendered, except in a matter in which a contingent fee is prohibited by paragraph (d) or other law. A contingent fee agreement shall be in a writing signed by the client and shall state the method by which the fee is to be determined, including the percentage or percentages that shall accrue to the lawyer in the event of settlement, trial or appeal; litigation and other expenses to be deducted from the recovery; and whether such expenses are to be deducted before or after the contingent fee is calculated. The agreement must clearly notify the client of any expenses for which the client will be liable whether or not the client is the prevailing party. Upon conclusion of a contingent fee matter, the lawyer shall provide the client with a written statement stating the outcome of the matter and, if there is a recovery, showing the remittance to the client and the method of its determination.

(d) A lawyer shall not enter into an arrangement for, charge, or collect:

(1) any fee in a domestic relations matter, the payment or amount of which is contingent upon the securing of a divorce or upon the amount of alimony or support, or property settlement in lieu thereof; or

(2) a contingent fee for representing a defendant in a criminal case.

(e) A division of a fee between lawyers who are not in the same firm may be made only if:

(1) the division is in proportion to the services performed by each lawyer or each lawyer assumes joint responsibility for the representation;

(2) the client agrees to the arrangement, including the share each lawyer will receive, and the agreement is confirmed in writing; and

(3) the total fee is reasonable.

▶ RULE 1.6 Confidentiality of Information

(a) A lawyer shall not reveal information relating to the representation of a client unless the client gives informed consent, the disclosure is impliedly authorized in order to carry out the representation or the disclosure is permitted by paragraph (b).

(b) A lawyer may reveal information relating to the representation of a client to the extent the lawyer reasonably believes necessary:

(1) to prevent reasonably certain death or substantial bodily harm;

(2) to prevent the client from committing a crime or fraud that is reasonably certain to result in substantial injury to the financial interests or property of another and in furtherance of which the client has used or is using the lawyer's services;

(3) to prevent, mitigate or rectify substantial injury to the financial interests or property of another that is reasonably certain to result or has resulted from the client's commission of a crime or fraud in furtherance of which the client has used the lawyer's services;

(4) to secure legal advice about the lawyer's compliance with these Rules;

(5) to establish a claim or defense on behalf of the lawyer in a controversy between the lawyer and the client, to establish a

defense to a criminal charge or civil claim against the lawyer based upon conduct in which the client was involved, or to respond to allegations in any proceeding concerning the lawyer's representation of the client; or

(6) to comply with other law or a court order.

▶ RULE 1.7   Conflict of Interest: Current Clients

(a) Except as provided in paragraph (b), a lawyer shall not represent a client if the representation involves a concurrent conflict of interest. Concurrent conflict of interest exists if:

(1) the representation of one client will be directly adverse to another client; or

(2) there is a significant risk that the representation of one or more clients will be materially limited by the lawyer's responsibilities to another client, a former client or a third person or by a personal interest of the lawyer.

(b) Notwithstanding the existence of a concurrent conflict of interest under paragraph (a), a lawyer may represent a client if:

(1) the lawyer reasonably believes that the lawyer will be able to provide competent and diligent representation to each affected client;

(2) the representation is not prohibited by law;

(3) the representation does not involve the assertion of a claim by one client against another client represented by the lawyer in the same litigation or other proceeding before a tribunal; and

(4) each affected client gives informed consent, confirmed in writing.

* * *

▶ Rule 1.13   Organization as Client

(a) A lawyer employed or retained by an organization represents the organization acting through its duly authorized constituents.

(b) If a lawyer for an organization knows that an officer, employee or other person associated with the organization is engaged in action, intends to act or refuses to act in a matter related to the representation that is a violation of a legal obligation to the organization, or a violation of law that reasonably might be imputed to the organization, and that is likely to result in substantial injury to the organization, then the lawyer shall proceed as is reasonably necessary in the best interest of the organization. Unless the lawyer reasonably believes that it is not necessary in the best interest of the organization to do so, the lawyer shall refer the matter to higher authority in the organization, including, if warranted by the circumstances, to the highest authority that can act on behalf of the organization as determined by applicable law.

(c) Except as provided in paragraph (d), if

(1) despite the lawyer's efforts in accordance with paragraph (b) the highest authority that can act on behalf of the organization insists upon or fails to address in a timely and appropriate manner an action, or a refusal to act, that is clearly a violation of law, and

(2) the lawyer reasonably believes that the violation is reasonably certain to result in substantial injury to the organization, then the lawyer may reveal information relating to the representation whether or not Rule 1.6 permits such disclosure, but only if and to the extent the lawyer reasonably

believes necessary to prevent substantial injury to the organization.

(d) Paragraph (c) shall not apply with respect to information relating to a lawyer's representation of an organization to investigate an alleged violation of law, or to defend the organization or an officer, employee or other constituent associated with the organization against a claim arising out of an alleged violation of law.

(e) A lawyer who reasonably believes that he or she has been discharged because of the lawyer's actions taken pursuant to paragraphs (b) or (c), or who withdraws under circumstances that require or permit the lawyer to take action under either of those paragraphs, shall proceed as the lawyer reasonably believes necessary to assure that the organization's highest authority is informed of the lawyer's discharge or withdrawal.

(f) In dealing with an organization's directors, officers, employees, members, shareholders or other constituents, a lawyer shall explain the identity of the client when the lawyer knows or reasonably should know that the organization's interests are adverse to those of the constituents with whom the lawyer is dealing.

(g) A lawyer representing an organization may also represent any of its directors, officers, employees, members, shareholders or other constituents, subject to the provisions of Rule 1.7. If the organization's consent to the dual representation is required by Rule 1.7, the consent shall be given by an appropriate official of the organization other than the individual who is to be represented, or by the shareholders.

* * *

▶ Rule 1.14   Client with Diminished Capacity

(a) When a client's capacity to make adequately considered decisions in connection with a representation is diminished, whether because of minority, mental impairment or for some other reason, the lawyer shall, as far as reasonably possible, maintain a normal client-lawyer relationship with the client.

(b) When the lawyer reasonably believes that the client has diminished capacity, is at risk of substantial physical, financial or other harm unless action is taken and cannot adequately act in the client's own interest, the lawyer may take reasonably necessary protective action, including consulting with individuals or entities that have the ability to take action to protect the client and, in appropriate cases, seeking the appointment of a guardian ad litem, conservator or guardian.

(c) Information relating to the representation of a client with diminished capacity is protected by Rule 1.6. When taking protective action pursuant to paragraph (b), the lawyer is impliedly authorized under Rule 1.6(a) to reveal information about the client, but only to the extent reasonably necessary to protect the client's interests.

* * *

▶ RULE 1.16   Declining or Terminating Representation

(a) Except as stated in paragraph (c), a lawyer shall not represent a client or, where representation has commenced, shall withdraw from the representation of a client if:

(1) the representation will result in violation of the Rules of Professional Conduct or other law;

(2) the lawyer's physical or mental condition materially impairs the lawyer's ability to represent the client; or

(3) the lawyer is discharged.

(b) Except as stated in paragraph (c), a lawyer may withdraw from representing a client if:

(1) withdrawal can be accomplished without material adverse effect on the interests of the client;

(2) the client persists in a course of action involving the lawyer's services that the lawyer reasonably believes is criminal or fraudulent;

(3) the client has used the lawyer's services to perpetrate a crime or fraud;

(4) the client insists upon taking action that the lawyer considers repugnant or with which the lawyer has a fundamental disagreement;

(5) the client fails substantially to fulfill an obligation to the lawyer regarding the lawyer's services and has been given reasonable warning that the lawyer will withdraw unless the obligation is fulfilled;

(6) the representation will result in an unreasonable financial burden on the lawyer or has been rendered unreasonably difficult by the client; or

(7) other good cause for withdrawal exists.

(c) A lawyer must comply with applicable law requiring notice to or permission of a tribunal when terminating a representation. When ordered to do so by a tribunal, a lawyer shall continue representation notwithstanding good cause for terminating the representation.

(d) Upon termination of representation, a lawyer shall take steps to the extent reasonably practicable to protect a client's interests, such as giving reasonable notice to the client, allowing time for employment of other counsel, surrendering papers and property to which the client is entitled and refunding any advance payment of fee or expense that has not been earned or incurred. The lawyer may retain papers relating to the client to the extent permitted by other law.

* * *

▶ RULE 2.1   Advisor

In representing a client, a lawyer shall exercise independent professional judgment and render candid advice. In rendering advice, a lawyer may refer not only to law but to other considerations such as moral, economic, social and political factors, that may be relevant to the client's situation.

* * *

▶ RULE 3.1   Meritorious Claims and Contentions

A lawyer shall not bring or defend a proceeding, or assert or controvert an issue therein, unless there is a basis in law and fact for doing so that is not frivolous, which includes a good faith argument for an extension, modification or reversal of existing law. A lawyer for the defendant in a criminal proceeding, or the respondent in a proceeding that could result in incarceration, may nevertheless so defend the proceeding as to require that every element of the case be established.

* * *

▶ RULE 3.3   Candor Toward the Tribunal

(a) A lawyer shall not knowingly:

    (1) make a false statement of fact or law to a tribunal or fail to correct a false statement of material fact or law previously made to the tribunal by the lawyer;

    (2) fail to disclose to the tribunal legal authority in the controlling jurisdiction known to the lawyer to be directly adverse to the position of the client and not disclosed by opposing counsel; or

    (3) offer evidence that the lawyer knows to be false. If a lawyer, the lawyer's client, or a witness called by the lawyer, has offered material evidence and the lawyer comes to know of its falsity, the lawyer shall take reasonable remedial measures, including, if necessary, disclosure to the tribunal. A lawyer may refuse to offer evidence, other than the testimony of a defendant in a criminal matter, that the lawyer reasonably believes is false.

(b) A lawyer who represents a client in an adjudicative proceeding and who knows that a person intends to engage, is engaging or has engaged in criminal or fraudulent conduct related to the proceeding shall take reasonable remedial measures, including, if necessary, disclosure to the tribunal.

(c) The duties stated in paragraphs (a) and (b) continue to the conclusion of the proceeding, and apply even if compliance requires disclosure of information otherwise protected by Rule 1.6.

(d) In an ex parte proceeding, a lawyer shall inform the tribunal of all material facts known to the lawyer that will enable the tribunal to make an informed decision, whether or not the facts are adverse.

▶ RULE 3.4   Fairness to Opposing Party and Counsel

A lawyer shall not:

(a) unlawfully obstruct another party's access to evidence or unlawfully alter, destroy or conceal a document or other material having potential evidentiary value. A lawyer shall not counsel or assist another person to do any such act;

(b) falsify evidence, counsel or assist a witness to testify falsely, or offer an inducement to a witness that is prohibited by law;

(c) knowingly disobey an obligation under the rules of a tribunal, except for an open refusal based on an assertion that no valid obligation exists;

(d) in pretrial procedure, make a frivolous discovery request or fail to make reasonably diligent effort to comply with a legally proper discovery request by an opposing party;

(e) in trial, allude to any matter that the lawyer does not reasonably believe is relevant or that will not be supported by admissible evidence, assert personal knowledge of facts in issue except when testifying as a witness, or state a personal opinion as to the justness of a cause, the credibility of a witness, the culpability of a civil litigant or the guilt or innocence of an accused; or

(f) request a person other than a client to refrain from voluntarily giving relevant information to another party unless:

(1) the person is a relative or an employee or other agent of a client; and

(2) the lawyer reasonably believes that the person's interests will not be adversely affected by refraining from giving such information.

▶ RULE 4.1 Truthfulness in Statements to Others

In the course of representing a client a lawyer shall not knowingly:

(a) make a false statement of material fact or law to a third person; or

(b) fail to disclose a material fact when disclosure is necessary to avoid assisting a criminal or fraudulent act by a client, unless disclosure is prohibited by Rule 1.6.

▶ RULE 4.3 Dealing with Unrepresented Person

In dealing on behalf of a client with a person who is not represented by counsel, a lawyer shall not state or imply that the lawyer is disinterested. When the lawyer knows or reasonably should know that the unrepresented person misunderstands the lawyer's role in the matter, the lawyer shall make reasonable efforts to correct the misunderstanding. The lawyer shall not give legal advice to an unrepresented person, other than the advice to secure counsel, if the lawyer knows or reasonably should know that the interests of such a person are or have a reasonable possibility of being in conflict with the interests of the client.

▶ Rule 5.1 Responsibilities of Partners, Managers, and Supervisory Lawyers

(a) A partner in a law firm, and a lawyer who individually or together with other lawyers possesses comparable managerial authority in a law firm, shall make reasonable efforts to ensure that the firm has in effect measures giving reasonable assurance that all lawyers in the firm conform to the Rules of Professional Conduct.

(b) A lawyer having direct supervisory authority over another lawyer shall make reasonable efforts to ensure that the other lawyer conforms to the Rules of Professional Conduct.

(c) A lawyer shall be responsible for another lawyer's violation of the Rules of Professional Conduct if:

> (1) the lawyer orders or, with knowledge of the specific conduct, ratifies the conduct involved; or

> (2) the lawyer is a partner or has comparable managerial authority in the law firm in which the other lawyer practices, or has direct supervisory authority over the other lawyer, and knows of the conduct at a time when its consequences can be avoided or mitigated but fails to take reasonable remedial action.

▸ Rule 5.2   Responsibilities of a Subordinate Lawyer

(a) A lawyer is bound by the Rules of Professional Conduct notwithstanding that the lawyer acted at the direction of another person.

(b) A subordinate lawyer does not violate the Rules of Professional Conduct if that lawyer acts in accordance with a supervisory lawyer's reasonable resolution of an arguable question of professional duty.

* * *

▸ RULE 5.4   Professional Independence of a Lawyer

(a) A lawyer or law firm shall not share legal fees with a nonlawyer, except that:

> (1) an agreement by a lawyer with the lawyer's firm, partner, or associate may provide for the payment of money, over a reasonable period of time after the lawyer's death, to the lawyer's estate or to one or more specified persons;

(2) a lawyer who purchases the practice of a deceased, disabled, or disappeared lawyer may, pursuant to the provisions of Rule 1.17, pay to the estate or other representative of that lawyer the agreed-upon purchase price;

(3) a lawyer or law firm may include nonlawyer employees in a compensation or retirement plan, even though the plan is based in whole or in part on a profit-sharing arrangement; and

(4) a lawyer may share court-awarded legal fees with a nonprofit organization that employed, retained or recommended employment of the lawyer in the matter.

▶ RULE 8.3 Reporting Professional Misconduct

(a) A lawyer who knows that another lawyer has committed a violation of the Rules of Professional Conduct that raises a substantial question as to that lawyer's honesty, trustworthiness or fitness as a lawyer in other respects, shall inform the appropriate professional authority.

(b) A lawyer who knows that a judge has committed a violation of applicable rules of judicial conduct that raises a substantial question as to the judge's fitness for office shall inform the appropriate authority.

(c) This Rule does not require disclosure of information otherwise protected by Rule 1.6 or information gained by a lawyer or judge while participating in an approved lawyers assistance program.

▶ RULE 8.4 Misconduct

It is professional misconduct for a lawyer to:

(a) violate or attempt to violate the Rules of Professional Conduct, knowingly assist or induce another to do so, or do so through the acts of another;

(b) commit a criminal act that reflects adversely on the lawyer's honesty, trustworthiness or fitness as a lawyer in other respects;

(c) engage in conduct involving dishonesty, fraud, deceit or misrepresentation;

(d) engage in conduct that is prejudicial to the administration of justice;

(e) state or imply an ability to influence improperly a government agency or official or to achieve results by means that violate the Rules of Professional Conduct or other law; or

(f) knowingly assist a judge or judicial officer in conduct that is a violation of applicable rules of judicial conduct or other law.

Time Sheet Entry

Attorney Name:

Client: Billing No.:

DATE	DESCRIPTION	TIME

Time Sheet Entry

Attorney Name:

Client: Billing No.:

DATE	DESCRIPTION	TIME

Time Sheet Entry

Attorney Name:

Client: Billing No.:

DATE	DESCRIPTION	TIME

Time Sheet Entry

Attorney Name:

Client: Billing No.:

DATE	DESCRIPTION	TIME

Time Sheet Entry

Attorney Name:

Client: Billing No.:

DATE	DESCRIPTION	TIME

Time Sheet Entry

Attorney Name:

Client: Billing No.:

DATE	DESCRIPTION	TIME

Time Sheet Entry

Attorney Name:

Client: Billing No.:

DATE	DESCRIPTION	TIME

Time Sheet Entry

Attorney Name:

Client: Billing No.:

DATE	DESCRIPTION	TIME

Time Sheet Entry

Attorney Name:

Client: Billing No.:

DATE	DESCRIPTION	TIME

Time Sheet Entry

Attorney Name:

Client: Billing No.:

DATE	DESCRIPTION	TIME

Time Sheet Entry

Attorney Name:

Client: Billing No.:

DATE	DESCRIPTION	TIME

Time Sheet Entry

Attorney Name:

Client: Billing No.:

DATE	DESCRIPTION	TIME